Away in a Manger

SONG LYRICS BY MARTIN LUTHER

ILLUSTRATED BY TERRY JULIEN

Published by Standard Publishing, Cincinnati, Ohio
www.standardpub.com

ISBN-13: 978-0-7847-1547-5
ISBN-10: 0-7847-1547-5

15 14 13 12 11 10   5 6 7 8 9 10 11 12 13

Standard® PUBLISHING

Cincinnati, Ohio

Away in a manger,
no crib for a bed,
The little Lord Jesus
laid down His sweet head;

The stars in the sky
looked down where He lay,

The little Lord Jesus,
asleep on the hay.

The cattle are lowing,
the baby awakes,
But little Lord Jesus,
no crying He makes.

I love Thee, Lord Jesus,
look down from the sky,

And stay by my cradle
till morning is nigh.

Be near me, Lord Jesus,
I ask Thee to stay
Close by me forever,
and love me I pray.

Bless all the dear children
in Thy tender care,
And take us to Heaven
to live with Thee there.